The 7 Principles for Strong Somalia

Abdiqani Farah

Copyright @ 2018 by Abdiqani Farah

Contents

Abdiqani Farah

DEDICATION

The 7 Principles of Strong Somalia is dedicated to those men and women who believe in Strong Somalia. It's for those rare types of Somalis who, whether in business, in government, or in non-governmental organizations, are committed to make Somalia great again.

Introduction

"To go wrong in one's own way is better than to go right in someone else's."

— Fyodor Dostoevsky, a Russian novelist, essayist, and philosopher

Welcome to what might be the most interesting and uplifting read so far into this year. The 7 Principles for Strong Somalia is a thought-provoking book. There are seven principles in this book, hence the 7 Principles. These principles represent the art of possibility and are worth trying.

This book seeks unapologetically a bottom-up political mobilization in Somalia—the world's most corruption-ravaged and neglected country. It's an advocate of politics run by Millennials and Generation X (those who were born between 1975 and 1999, respectively), those men and women of great characters anywhere in the world.

If the *Prince* was written for those who have power and want to protect it, the 7 Principles for Strong Somalia was written for those exceptional young people who aspire to power through good governance and democratic process. If Niccolo Machiavelli wrote the Prince for cold-blooded dictators of any century, this book was written for those who sit on the other side of the spectrum.

Machiavelli's intention in Prince reflected the 1500 Europe, and his theories were rooted in handling the exercise of raw power toward unquestioned dynasties. Machiavelli suggested inherently sophisticated tactics for grabbing power, and holding onto it, an awful advice meant to suppress the mass for complete control.

Conversely, this book is for those young, educated Somalis who sympathize with the ideals of liberty, freedom, and equality for all before the law. I don't entertain manipulative actions, and never will I advise you to. Rest assured, the principles in this book aren't based on hunger for power and don't lead to dictatorship, but to good governance and bottom-up accountability.

Characteristically, the 7 Principles for Strong Somalia is for those young people embody the optimism of tribal-free Somalia and have the capacity to collectively pursue progressive social politics. But despite the limited resources and opportunities to try out their ideas on the political marketplace, they're bound by facial, tribal boundaries.

The 7 Principles for Strong Somalia provides them with the opportunity to try out their ideas. The objectives of this book are an upward social democracy and civic involvement based on sustainable development.

Regardless of where they're at this point in time, their status in their communities, where they're born and to which family, their schooling and social upbringing, the 7 Principles for Strong Somalia is a practical, fast-written approach to social politics.

Let me be honest with you here. I've not held a political office, and I'm not interested in running for an office either. I even hate politics. But I've a passion to take part in the rebuilding of Somalia, not as a politician but as a citizen. I've been following the politics of Somalia since 2000, and with a keen interest to understand every political action and behavior in the realm of the Horn of African politics.

I've also read the biographies of many prominent military and civilian leaders, as well as contemporary thought leaders. Some of the leaders whose ideas you'll encounter in the book attained power through compassionate leadership and all-out love for their countries and constitutions. Most of these leaders left office with a higher approval rating. Leaving office with a higher rating shows a positive sign of likeability and public approval. The 44th U.S. President Barack Obama is an example. Obama's public approval rating was 62 percent the day before Donald Trump was elected president. Obama wasn't without critics. Despite the mounting pressure surrounding a black man in the most powerful office in the world, he earned the respect of well-mannered people throughout the world.

The Seven Principles

This book contains seven principles that I believe can help statesmen/women to pioneer a social and political change in the Horn of Africa. Setting the stage for the rest of the principles, the first principle discusses the importance of self-determination and independence. Self-determination, as a cornerstone of any successful nation, is the core determinant of the goals nations pursue. This principle shows you how to reverse the lack of self-determination in Somalia in common hours. The second principle follows directly from the first principle and advocates for a win-win interaction with the wider world. The third principle talks about how social democracy and civic involvement can replace the current anarchy in Somalia. The fourth principle functions as a way to measure progress; it details how to set ambitious, measurable goals for the country. The fifth principle sheds light on how to rebuild and restore Somalia's foreign service reputation. The sixth principle deals with a major problem that appears on your way as soon as you enter politics. That ugly elephant is tribalism, and this principle shows you how to deal with it effectively without losing your sanity. Finally, the seventh principle shows you how to become an ethical leader.

With all these, I'm not here to say that I've all the answers to Somalia's problems. Far from it. These principles are gleaned from my understanding of this century's social politics, and they present the beginning of one man's approach to his country's social, political, and economic ills. I could be wrong, but stand guilty as charged whenever I'm proven as such. After all, as the quote at the beginning of this introduction shows, it's always better to sail off with a map of your own than to sail with someone else's plan. I would rather be wrong in my own way than to wait for a ghost to come and fix my own problems. I want to die believing knowingly that I did all I could. What about you?

I made the book short, even shorter so that readers can go through it in a matter of days, or weeks. Because it's a guide, I chose the principles to be handy for quick application. In fact, it was my intention to help the reader to get the essence of the book in a single shot and digest the information while also juggling other matters. I also tried to make it as humorous as possible, while embedding valuable, practical and fast-acting information.

How to Approach the Book

You can approach the book in many ways. You can read it in sequence, or at random, going straight to the chapters you feel the most urge for. You can also read those chapters that you might need to review as you go about and tackle your day-to-day activities. There are stand-alone quotes intended to serve as lampposts and principles to implement as you need them. Better yet, you can use a notepad to transfer ideas for quick application. No matter your approach, the book will keep you inspired and stay focused.

In fact, the book can be your go-to advisor. You can keep it by your bedside, if you've a hardcopy, and consult the particular readings based on the questions you might have when you retire into the night, or as you sip your coffee on your way to work. If you're using it on your electronic device, you can also put a copy on the screen so you can access it for faster look-up for ideas. Whenever you feel tired and/or bombarded with hostile-looking issues, you can detach yourself from the situation and return to your confidential advisor.

Anything is possible if you are willing to pay the price.

I want to conclude the introduction with a warning! In politics, as in life, the problems that can cause you to fall and fail are many, and the obstacles in your way even enormously great. I want you to remember that nothing great has been achieved without challenges and obstacles. Fortunately, and with persistence and continuous perfection on your part, the principles in this book can help you in building a competitive nation which commands respect and trust at home and abroad. And as Benjamin Hardy, an organizational psychologist, observed, "anything is possible if you are willing to pay the price."

Have fun and let's begin.

Principle

1

Self-determination and independence are key for a successful Somalia.

"Self-determination is not a mere phrase. It is an imperative principle of action, which statesmen will henceforth ignore at their peril."

— Woodrow Wilson, the 28th U.S. President

With your indulgence, allow me to start the chapter with a short story. Not long ago, Abdullahi Sultan, a friend of mine, met a white man while riding a bus in Seattle, Washington. Abdullahi and the white had had an interesting conversation, touching one of the most interesting sociopolitical affairs of our time: Why the black people are on the periphery of the economic ladder.

In an attempt to make his point clearer, the white man told a story about three men (an African, a white, and an Arab). One day, the three men decided to go to God and ask for his abundance. The promise was that the men's individual request would be readily accepted if they approached God honestly and straightforwardly and boldly placed their request before him.

But the men had to agree on the order in which they'd meet God. According to the white man who told the story, the guests agreed to meet God in this order: The white man would go first, then the Arab, then the African. When the white man met God, he bravely asked for the secret keys to the world: education, technology, intelligence, influence, etc. Then the Arab man's turn came. When he met God, the Arab asked for oil monopoly so he could supply it to the world for profit, and hence creating leverage and strength. Lastly, the

African man's turn arrived. When there, God asked, "what do you want?" Hesitant and wandering, the African told God that he was accompanying the other two men. He wanted nothing! It turned out that the African man had no aspirations and ambitions in life and had to be tossed away, as a result.

What is the moral of the story? My understanding of the story is that Africans suffer from a lack of self-determination and the propensity to own their future and leave a legacy. Lack of ambition keeps the black people on the periphery of today's competitive world. It's the very reason that the African continent is in poverty, protracted civil war, and intellectual inertia. Unlike other people, the inhabitants of the African continent have no idea why they're here on earth.

This is even worse for Somalia. Instead of thinking critically and going after big goals, we settled for the mediocre. We unconsciously wrote off our self-determination and independence and, as a result, remained poor and dependent on others. We mistakenly believe that some other people, certainly not us, are responsible for our future.

We bought into the notion of entitlement; that those who were given the oil and the keys to the world owe us everything. We became satisfied with the western aid, and the sadaqah, the voluntary charity that Arabs give the poorer Muslims. That's why Somalia has been in a dare situation for a long time, still believing some other nations are coming to its rescue. We've no clue why God brought us here.

Somalia has been, and still is, on the periphery of a fast-growing world in which economy and technology are the core driving forces of modern life. It's been dependent on foreign aid. In fact, it's the only nation that can't fix the sewage system of its state house and parliamentary buildings without seeking the help of funders.

Unfortunately, the universal principles that govern the world don't work that way. God put us on earth not to beg others but to prosper in our own right. Every newborn baby, male or female, comes to the world with the most powerful human machine ever built, the brain and its wiring system. We were designed to get what we work for tirelessly, and day-in and day-out.

We should understand that all people, black or brown, white or red, were created equal and that no one was given the responsibility for the bread of others. We're created equal, and responsible for whatever happens, or doesn't happen, to us. Needlessly, the former U.S. President Barack Obama, who never shied away from engaging in such ideas during his presidency, emphasized this point. Speaking at a commencement at Morehouse College, Obama told the new graduates: "Nobody is going to give you anything that you have not earned."

Self-determination, the desire for a great nationhood, isn't given; it's earned. There's no excuse for inaction and dependence on aid. A decision to decide the right course for Somalia is going to have to be made, and time is of the essence.

> **Nobody is going to give you anything that you have not earn.**

Instead of being dependent on others, we've to work from the mindset of contributing to the world, or better yet, leading the world in today's most important fronts. And what's wrong with Somalia leading the world in technology and nuclear physics? That's achievable.

Sadly, politicians in Somalia operate from a mindset of dependency and complacency, that the world owes us everything. That's why Somalia has been a giant recipient of foreign aid, since the collapse of the last central government. Statistically speaking, Somalia received $55 billion in aid between 1991 and 2011, according to Center for American Progress. Somalia was also reported to have received an additional $1.3 billion in humanitarian aid between 2011 and 2016. That totals to $56.3 billion, not to mention the hundreds of millions of dollars in remittance each year. How much would each person receive if we took the conservative population estimate of 15.2 million people and tried to distribute that amount to all Somalis equally?

Well, these statistics shouldn't scare us. The numbers are here for us to reflect upon and change them if we don't like them. Why can't we change the situation? History taught us that Somalia can reverse the current status quo of dependence.

Sure, Somalia still needs the help of other nations, but that need shouldn't stand between the nation and its desire to self-determination and independence. Somalia can still ask for help, but should be mindful of the consequences of the help it gets. Somalia shouldn't be owned through sadaqah.

The thing is, our leaders aren't comfortable with the ugly truth: Aid isn't a viable exit out of poverty; on the contrary, aid is the main highway that leads to poverty. For a strong Somalia, carefully projected national development initiatives are crucial.

The Marshall Plan for Somalia

A sustainable development plan that can look a win-win to other nations is more important than any foreign sadaqah! Maybe something like the Marshall Plan of 1948, in which the U.S. pledged more $12 billion of economic assistance to rebuild Western Europe after World War II, will work for Somalia.

But for a huge bailout like the Marshall Plan requires a lot more than most politicians in Mogadishu are willing to realize. This is especially true for Somalia whose record is tainted with corruption and human rights malpractices. Transparency International ranked Somalia, in its 2017 Corruption Index, as the most corrupt country in the globe. On a scale of zero to a hundred, "where 0 is highly corrupt and 100 is very clean," Somalia's score is nine (9). Actually, Somalia is the only country with a single digit score. New Zealand lies at the other extreme and was ranked number one least corrupt nation on that index, with a score of 89.

The recipients of the Marshall Plan of 1948 all understood the importance of an economic plan. Austria, France, Ireland, Italy, Netherlands, Portugal, and Sweden were recipient nations of the Marshall Plan. Every single of one these nations had a good understanding of their particular circumstances, and what they had to achieve with the plan. They rebuilt their nations fast, immediately joined other economically developed nations, and started to attract economic immigrants from other parts of the world, especially Africa and Asia. Only self-determination could make that possible.

Like the recipients of the Marshall Plan, Somalia must be able to show where the money will go. Rules that can govern a huge bailout like the Marshall Plan have to be put in place if Somalia is going to pursue economic investments over aid. This is because a good economic plan requires adequate measures of accountability and transparency. Admittedly, a sound governance system with transparency and accountability is going to be a mandatory part of any economic deal.

The current rampant corruption has to be mitigated before the world can offer Somalia a sound rebuilding plan. Those nations Somalia is courting for help will need to see how the aid will have to be used. The impact of the foreign help must be substantiated before and after the plan is complete. Until that system is in place, Somalia will go from conference to another with zero impact.

The point of self-determination is this: Somalia is better off projecting a respectable image rather than begging, with or without economic assistance. It must look like an equal partner in the world of nations. Instead of begging, it should think of borrowing from richer but inertia-infected nations. Indeed, that's what most of the developed countries do. For example, as of 2016, U.S. owes Saudi Arabia a nearly $117 billion, according to the U.S. Treasury. Why not borrow money and attract long-term investment projects?

> **If you're not at the table, you're on the menu.**

The same Saudi Arabia is going to tell Somalia that it's un-Islamic and technically forbidden, to borrow money on interest rates. Yet, Saudi Arabia is happy to send political money to Somalia in order to topple the government. Understand: Saudi Arabia isn't happy with self-determined, successful Somalia.

Yes, we can. But for that to happen, Somalia has to look like an equal partner at the table, with respect and resolve before the world can take it seriously. In other words, "if you're not at the table, you're on the menu." If Somalia wants to be a beggar and has nothing offer the world, it'll be unable to assertively have a say at the table. It'll most likely be served not only abroad but at home, and do you know what other nations have for Somalia? Probably not much.

All responsible nations understand that aid doesn't lead to independence. When you're the beneficiary of the developmental programs of any foreign nation, those who offer you these benefits will have to get their interests met. That, sure, creates a sort of unavoidable dependence and continuation of power and political inequality. You just can't be dependent on aid and other forms of assistance and expect independence and self-determination.

It all comes down to the principle of this chapter: self-determination and independence are key for a successful nation. A national determination and a constitution that guarantees equal rights before the law can create a power balance in the most unequal political equations. If Somalia wants to succeed, the culture of being dependent on aid needs to be reversed.

Nations develop, fail to develop, or even disappear from the face of the earth, based on what their people do, or don't do. In fact, no country has ever reached an optimal peak of nationhood without citizens who could take pride in the existence of their country and work hard to achieve a better status. From economy to education to military to public service, democracy has taken a deeper root in nations where citizens single-handedly choose to stand up and confront the challenges of their time.

The Independence

Luckily, Somalia traveled the path of self-determination before and can do it again. We've seen an unwavering national determination during the struggle for independence in the 1950s. In the fight to depose the British and the Italian occupiers, the Somali Youth League (SYL) showed an extraordinary bravery and sacrifice and helped sow a sense of self-determination in the Somali people.

For starters, SYL didn't have the luxury of technological advances, nor a nuclear capability to scare off the conquistadors and decisively win the war. Their communication channels were often disrupted by rain, by an enemy ambush or by superior military deceptions. Yet, they did the job well. Fortunately, they did have what it took at the time to build a coherent nation: a national pledge toward self-determination. That's a debt none of us will be able to repay.

The same thing could be said of other struggles in Africa. At independence, the Mau Mau fighters in Kenya carry the same spirit and managed to bring home the long-awaited victory.

The power of that self-determination can still do all the difference in Somalia. But we're going to have to think differently.

The idea is simple. God doesn't care whether we're black or white. God cares whether we can come across as bold and responsible humans. God cares whether we can determine our destiny and follow through with action and resolve. Needlessly, God helps those who are self-determined and want independence so badly.

Self-determination is an expression of the individual and collective right to democracy.

Now, all of us have one obligation: to continue the business SYL started and died for. We can do so by playing our respective roles in the rebuilding of a great Somalia. Some may mobilize communities and others may contribute to the economy by conducting investment in people and infrastructure. And yet others may be called to serve and run for offices. My role in the rebuilding is to re-emphasize the SYL's euphoria of self-determination and independence, by sharing with you this book. Whatever our respective roles, we must come forward and serve the nation gracefully. In the end, we'll have individual endeavors and collective action toward the betterment of Somalia. And as the American lawyer, writer, and historian, Alfred-Maurice de Zayas, wrote, "self-determination is an expression of the individual and collective right to democracy."

All self-determined nations understand the importance of making bold strides toward the unknown and the change to risk something, providing their people with a better future. Instead of embracing the road to foreign aid and dependability, excuses and waiting for the rest of the world to rescue them, determined nations choose the path of developments and risk-taking through investment. Responsible nations understand that excuses lead to nothing but a national demise. That's the ultimate power of self-determination and independence.

We Don't Deserve Lies

Conversely, most poor nations tend to underestimate the power of national confidence. They believe in the wrong version of social lifestyle and democracy. They erroneously think that the development of the poor is the job of those with the means. And that one way to secure the favor of the big nations is to give up the power to self-determination.

Because of that regressionist mindset, leaders in Africa oppress their people through imprisonment and state-owned propaganda apparatus against those who speak of the truth. They portray a misleading picture of their nation on the global stage by telling made-up stories that have no grounding at home. They tell their international audiences how democratic Africa is growing, while deception, imprisonment, suppression of the press, and other forms of harsh treatments are the order of the day.

That's true in Somalia where leaders can't face national challenges squarely in the eye. For example, leaders say, at least on camera, that citizens are going to cast their votes in the next election. They told people exactly that when the elections of 2012 and 2016 were merely six months away. Everybody knew that that wasn't going to happen anytime soon. In fact, the odds are stacked against the possibility of popular elections in which citizens can vote before 2040.

Truly, popular elections aren't going to happen until the following fundamentals are met: freedom of the press; freedom to form and belong to associations; unbiased, non-politicized judicial powers; and constant debates of current policies and the constitution by anyone willing to come forward. And none of these is possible until a clear national course has been set.

Getting people to do adaptive work is the mark of leadership in a competitive world.

Sure, free and fair electoral process is the beginning of self-determination. But people are going to have to be part of the process of rebuilding the nation. You can't decide a nation's destiny behind closed doors, albeit committed leadership is paramount in setting the national stage for success. In a Harvard Business Review article, Ronald Heifetz and Donald Laurie argued that "getting people to do adaptive work is the mark of leadership in a competitive world." In short, people must be part of the initial process.

Lies and manipulative ways to control people don't help you with the necessary buy-in for self-determination. When the legitimacy of the government fades away, whatever leaders tell their people is registered as a mock in the minds of the people. No world power can help you to regain a lost trust. Arguably, therefore, collective self-determination grows when democracy takes root in communities and in neighborhoods.

Empower Citizens

Self-determined democracies focus on empowering their citizens. They set policies and issue executive orders to make sure that all citizens are tuned in. Because empowered citizens are in a good position to make their own laws, the resultant government is run by the collective will of the people. Leaders are mere facilitators of the process. That means that the president, the speaker, senators, or any other office holder must get the approval of the majority public. To put it straight, the complete ins and outs of the government must be subject to the approval of the public. This is a collective self-determination in its retail form.

In order for Somalia to re-emerge, leaders must single-mindedly pursue agendas expected to advance the interests of the people of Somalia, no matter the situation. They must always be tuned in the "what's-in-it-for-us" mindset.

Of course, to secure longer-term interests, Somalia may be forced to leave an important position, and to cooperate with the rest of the world. But, inevitably, national policies should be the nation's core guiding compass. To build a great nation doesn't happen in a vacuum; it involves setting goals and pursuing these goals to the finish line.

In sum, self-determination doesn't mean a total disregard of globalization. Globalization and self-determination aren't incompatible, and nations can be both self-determined and globalization-conscious. Actually, only when a nation embraces an absolute direction of self-determination can it also respond to global issues that require international cooperation. Globalization, in its most basic form, therefore, is to have an unwavering degree of commitment and respect for international laws and culture. Somalia can be the most democratic, have a noble respect for the international treaties, and yet be a determined nation in its own right.

It's better to face your problems head on, decisively, instead of fooling yourself.

Somalia's problem isn't about a bad economy, nor is it about piracy; it's about the lack of self-determination. It, therefore, behooves young politicians to rethink the old way of doing business and to pursue agendas that can help the nation with the much-needed self-determination. We must collectively face challenges head on, so next generations will have something to work on. And as Laura Mintegi put it unequivocally in her book, Nerea and I, "it's better to face your problems head on, decisively, instead of fooling yourself."

Yes, we can.

Principle

2

Drop the victim mindset and embrace win-win with the wider world.

"It is mutual trust, even more than mutual interest, that holds human associations together."

— Henry Louis Mencken, an American journalist, satirist, cultural critic, and scholar

The 7.5-billion-plus people are united by an increasingly integrated technology. A teenager in Trinidad and Tobacco can make an instant connection and hang out virtually with another teenager in East Timor. What binds these teenagers together is the internet connection and the electronic devices in their hands. In fact, I'm prepared to bet that you're reading this book on a handheld device, an advancement completely unthinkable in the 1990s.

If this trend has any meaning and relevance for Somalia, it's this: Technology is disrupting our way of life. Technology is shaping not only the way that we view the world, but how we should associate with other people, and even how we cook our food and eat.

We've become one human tribe united by common reality, common cultures and common goals. Put it this way, if you're born in the 1980s or late '90s, the chances are that you've friends in all corners of the world. What's so unique and special about your connection with the world is that we all matter, and that we all have a common destiny that we're all prepared to defend.

The world is getting heavily interdependent, with more and more people, organizations and governments connecting with each other to solve common problems.

It's brought the world a lot closer together and will continue to do that.

Before the internet disruption in the 1990s, governments controlled the media, and what people said through media with an iron fist. Oppressive governments were able to regulate their port of entries, shutting down border crossings just to prevent the smuggling of foreign ideas into their countries. For instance, if a merchant in the U.S. sold an item to a Russian consumer during the Cold War, she'd find an FBI team in her living room the next day. That's how bad things were before the connected world.

But that era is over, and the world has gotten tinier and internet-run, creating a borderless, interdependence in the process. Speaking of technology, Steve Jobs said: "I think it's brought the world a lot closer together and will continue to do that." It's naive and virtually counterproductive to think otherwise.

Understand: The world has changed, and so must we.

Today, ideas are getting borderless, and governments less in control. Oppression was replaced by open borders, open laws, open societies, open-minds, and common reality driven by real human feelings. This isn't a cliche but a fact that you must accept and embrace. People in different parts of the world can easily watch the average breakfast of other people, rich or poor, including those who live under most tyrant regimes. We're witnessing Thomas Friedman' predictions. In the World is Flat, Friedman prophesied that the whole would be an even playing field for everyone who's willing to participate.

This necessitated the need for an ever-deepening dependence on one another, global interdependence, and the need for mutual relationships among different people and states in different geographical locations. Wholly diverse groups are working on issues that were once the problems of a particular region or state. This fact forced governments to respond openly and courageously to social demands of flat borders. More and more groups with different missions are coming together to face the common challenges of today: closing socioeconomic gaps and eradicating poverty.

The Political Actors

Across Somalia, there are diverse actors, all wanting to contribute to greater Somalia. These actors include international organizations, local organizations, community groups, and academic institutions. The common aim of all of these organizations is to promote a safer environment for all to grow and to reach their potential. The underlying philosophy behind what these actors do whirls around multilateral interests. In short, you can't just pretend to be living in today's flattened world and still avoid joining hands with those actors who are working to better the lives of those you claim to represent. If Somalia is willing to win and thrive in the long run, it has no option to build the right environment for these different actors.

In addition to the indulging differences that people tend to have, the world has many intersecting interests and goals that are harder to achieve unilaterally. In fact, there are challenges that Somalia isn't prepared to face alone, forcing the need for alliances and relationships based on mutual interest and mutual gain.

Most developed democracies are rethinking their public policies and revisiting constitutions and national charters. They're doing so to accommodate the diverse needs of globally interlinked societies.

What does that mean for Somalia? It means embracing a fairer, democratic, and hospitable relationship with the rest of the world. That means creating the right environment for that interest to materialize. Somalia is going to have to undertake policy measures that promote not only businesses and economic infrastructures but the interests of all concerned parties.

The era when the most powerful gets the most out of every opportunity is long done. Now we're in the era of honesty, trust, mutual interest, and shared values. And those with the right tools who are able to accommodate the interests of others are far more likely to succeed and develop their nations faster.

But wait! Haven't I said in the preceding chapter that self-determination is important? Yes, but understanding how the world has changed will help Somalia making it big. This is, by no means, a way to relinquish Somalia's sovereignty and independence, or your responsibility to your nation. Somalia will be in a better position when we drop the victim mindset, read the world with a healthy lens, and embrace comparative advantage.

What's more, alliances and partnerships don't mean dominance and a recipe for manipulation. Realistically, interest-based friendship doesn't mean sacrificing independence and self-determination. It means opportunities for both the weaker and stronger. It's a matter of striking a balance between your strategic goals and ambitions and the strategic goals of others.

The Self-Defeating Theory

Sadly, there's a profound conspiracy theory floating in social discussions, across Somalia, that the country has been taken hostage by foreign governments under the auspices of aid agencies. This theory is based on the idea that "there's no free lunch on Wall Street."

Most of the arguments around this theory come down one question: Why are Western organizations spending millions of dollars on Somalia if they've no ulterior motive? Perhaps, they want to steal the country's resources! some may assert. To them, it's as though the country has been hijacked by foreigners, not at a gunpoint but through money and invisible propaganda. Some took the issue too far by saying that all international NGOs are spies and snooping entities and shouldn't be trusted.

Another equally self-defeating thinking is the false sense of entitlement. Many believe mistakenly that, for Somalia to come back on its feet, the international community has the obligation to help. That's an absurdly backward-thinking, at best, and dependence mindset at worst. That needs to be rethought.

My word to those folks who entertain this idea is this: No one is here to take your country; your thinking takes you to that dark alley. You're sidetracked by your own thinking and phony political controversies.

In fact, holding such negativity may lead Somalia to further problems down the road as the country fights its way to greatness. Negative attitudes will only lead to self-destructing behavior and isolation. As a leader, you must never entertain these cheap conspiracy theories and pedestrian thinking. Better yet, you can gain a lot by approaching these political controversies with a positive attitude.

I'm persuaded that those who are attracted to this theory have misread the new world. They're still in a survival-of-the-fittest mode. And by default, they're creating more negativity than they're trying to solve. The real question they should be asking is how to capitalize on the millions of dollars that go to Somalia and use them to rebuild the nation?

No doubt, the international organizations working in Somalia are there to help the people of Somalia in realizing their potential and producing the best they can. They brought the much-needed assistance, but it's up to the Somalis to take advantage of the hand extended to them.

The Isolationist Mindset

Victim mindset is the mother of isolation, mistrust, and underdevelopment. Isolation is dangerous, and political isolations are seriously deadly. An isolated nation can't get ahead, nor can it feed its people. Take the Islamic Republic of Iran, for instance. Iran couldn't move fast, even though Iranians seem to be the most committed people on the planet. Their ego-feeding desire for nuclear power and dominance blinded Iranians to shift their mindset. Having a national ego, or pursuing a nuclear ambition, is a good deal, but nuclear programs can't be a substitute for food in a country, like Somalia, where poverty continues to threaten the lives of thousands of people.

Social and economic isolations lead nations to an unrecoverable trauma and psychological defeat. Understand: An isolated enemy is quite predictable and vulnerable to all sorts of irritations than an enemy interacted with. The latter will keep your weapons ready because you can anticipate the moves of your enemies and countermoves as they carry out their activities and entice you into action. More so, if an organization is suspected of engaging in espionage activities, it's always better to interact with that organization and to understand its motives from inside out than left alone.

The victim mindset—that the world is doing Somalia harm—will only send a negative ripple effect in no time. As the quote at the beginning of the chapter shows, Robert Greene's Law 18 of the 48 laws of power concluded the downside of isolation eloquently. Greene proved historically that isolation hastened the downfall of powerful kings and courtiers. "Isolation exposes you to more dangers than it protects you from," he wrote. There's nothing to be gained from building an inward fortress of mistrust, but everything to be gained from collaboration for the better.

Isolation exposes you to more dangers than it protects you from.

I believe that Jiddu Krishnamurti, an Indian philosopher and writer, put this point better. He said: "You may withdraw into the mountains, become a monk, a sannyasi, wander off into the desert by yourself, but you are related. You cannot escape from that absolute fact. You cannot exist in isolation." In a word, you can always do better by collaborating with all actors, including those with whom you disagree.

You cannot exist in isolation.

Suspicion and isolation are no longer the right strategies. Harboring old negative thinking in this increasingly interdependent world will never be productive. A viable strategy is a collaboration and synergy, and Somalia is better off dropping the victim mindset and embracing win-win with the wider world. If Somalia has any chance to recover from the mess of the civil war, political actors would need to embrace a new way of thinking.

Really, what is the world getting out of Somalia, even if destructive activities are proved to be happening? What do you've to lose? Somalia has already in a disadvantageous position, regardless of how much oil, gas, minerals, and untapped resources there is! Somalia has already secured an unfavorable status: the world's most failed state, located in the world's most uncertain territory. What the hell do you've to lose? As a leader, you're better off collaborating, giving up some share of the untapped resources so you can deal with poverty first and put the country onto the fast track of development.

If you want to help your nation reach its potential, there're going to have to be a mindset rework. This is particularly true when people are living at the lower end of the human transaction and are constantly buying into the victim's mindset.

Above all, be the heroine of your life, not the victim.

As a leader, you've the responsibility to reverse all the negative thinking in the political and social markets across the country. Instead of looking like a victim and entertaining self-defeating thoughts, you can go to work and be your own hero or heroine, and for those millions of hopeless people. Let the American journalist, writer, and filmmaker, Nora Ephron, once said, "above all, be the heroine of your life, not the victim" be your heroine.

Take 100% Responsibility

Dropping the victim mindset requires taking 100 percent responsibility for rethinking Somalia's relationship with the world. Think about it. If you and your neighbors are working on the same project and serving the same locality, isn't it a better idea to relate better to these stakeholders, and join in hands with them to serve your communities even better? Your answer to this question is, I believe, a resounding "yes." More so if you're willing to serve, you should also be willing to collaborate with those who are dealing with the same issues and serving the same audiences.

For Somalia, collaboration means combining synergies in a forceful way, helping all parties benefit in the process. By collaborating and partnering with others on issues that matter to you both, you create a synergy and the collective power to accomplish so much in less time.

Taking complete responsibility for reshaping Somalia's future is a cause worth pursuing. If suspicion and mistrust can't prove a viable strategy, why don't you try the opposite? Instead of harboring suspicion, why not open up business opportunities for conglomerates and investors who might help you with resources you need to rebuild the country?

If the economically developed nations have the capital and technology to invest, why not let them in and have their share of the prospect? They've the means: the technology, money, the know-how that you need to potentially turn your country into a developed nation in less time. The unique needs each of powerful partners creates avenues of opportunities for the poor, as these able partners bring something tangible to the table.

The most successful political entrepreneurs are those who open all investors and intellectual communities to their shores, and for the benefit of all. In sum, both Somalia and partners gain. That's possible when Somalia embraces a win-win for all and changes from victim mindset to a winner's mindset. The rule of thumb is, therefore, this: There's no place for cynical thinking if you want to transform your nation into an economic powerhouse.

If you mean business, you're better off dropping the victim mindset of the accuser and the accused and getting down to business. Hop on the bus that you live in an increasingly interconnected world where national borders and nationalist policies, and the depreciating values that drove political dominance for centuries, are threatened by the technology-driven democracy of the mass, the urge to remove the artificial fences that previous generations built.

Collaborative relationships with all social actors will be crucial, and trust will further deepen your relationships. Brian Tracy observed, "the glue that holds all relationships together—including the relationship between the leader and the led—is trust, and trust is based on integrity."

> **The glue that holds all relationships together is trust, and trust is based on integrity.**

Finally, a world based on trust and mutual interest is a world based on win-win. All partnerships are based on pursuing common objectives. While there are ample opportunities to make policy shifts and embrace risk, unstable policies can impede your progress toward strong Somalia. Put differently, moving between alliances will make you both unpredictable and unreliable. Actually, going between Saudi Arabia, Qatar,

Turkey, the EU, and the U.S. is a political suicide.

However, there are times when the interest of foreigners may not be accommodated and considered. But overall, cooperating with all relevant partners can prove Somalia's success. Your tendency to embrace on the less traveled road can infuriate your alliances and neighbors; that's to be expected. Your enemies will increase when you declare your ambition to fix Somalia's problems.

As a matter of fact, the harder you pursue uncommon dreams, the lesser your circle. That must never lower ambition. That's the way it's, has always been, and it'll always be. Be prepared for this eventuality. You must never betray your alliances.

Proceed forward, the world is yours.

Principle

3

The pathway to social democracy in Somalia is civic involvement.

"There are three critical ingredients to democratic renewal and progressive change: good public policy, grassroots organizing and electoral politics."

Abdiqani Farah

— Paul Wellstone, an academic, author and U.S. Senator from 1991-2002

The key concept in this chapter isn't democracy; it's civic awareness. In the social realm, the concepts of democracy and civic awareness are interchangeable. One is a means to a goal; the other an end. But both disciplines require common objectives that a nation may want to achieve, no matter the leverage.

This chapter starts off by emphasizing the fact that civic awareness is a means to a democracy. It's a way to ignite the awareness of community organizing—the art of civic politics. If politics is the art of possibility, community organizing is a fuel for a democratic society. That is, civic awareness is a vehicle to civic participation in politics and the mechanism to successful social democracy.

Community organizing is all about building grassroots support. It's about identifying the people around you.

But in order to organize your community and your neighbors, you must have a passion for it. Top Peters, a community organizing expert, argued that community organizing should be based on building social change initiatives on "a common, passionate cause." It's that common passion that fuels the powerful movements of this century. According to Peters, therefore, "community organizing is all about building grassroots support. It's about identifying the people around you with whom you can create a common, passionate cause."

In its basic form, community organizing is creating a platform for those common dreams and pains people share, even when they're not organized. You must be able to harness the power of communities which, organized around common compassion, can fuel a street-based love for the common good.

Building social change initiatives on a common, passionate cause.

Community organizing functions as a check and balance mechanism that regulates what politicians in state capitals do. It's a way of organizing people for shared governance, regulating the actions and behaviors of selfish politicians.

Community organizing is the heart and soul of any progressive politics in which the ordinary people have a decision in the direction of their government. It's crucial for a mature democracy.

So principally, without the people having a say in the direction their country should go, Somalia will always entertain the dictatorship style of the 19th century. And the government will always listen to the guy with the most coins in the pocket. Community organizing, done for the sole purpose of civic participation in politics, is going to be key for Somalia to see the light of healthy social democracy. In other words, the pathway to social democracy starts with organized communities wanting to perfect their lives through organized initiatives.

But we must not confuse community organizing with political canvassing. While these terms might sound to refer to the same thing, they're indeed worlds apart. On the one hand, the objective in community organizing is to create an awareness among people, so they stand for up for their rights. Canvassing, on the other hand, is an active campaign intended to call attention to a candidate or a cause, ultimately leading to a vote. In community organizing, people own the platform; in canvassing, the politician seeking our votes owns it.

Both practical politics and academic science have proved that the power of community organizing can decisively tilt the odds in our favor, changing the political landscape forever.

Governance is a way of organizing, amplifying, and constraining power.

The combination of science and practice concluded that community organizing is the route to complete civic awareness and accountable governance.

In fact, as Rebecca MacKinnon put it, to organize people is the objective of governance. She wrote: "Governance is a way of organizing, amplifying, and constraining power." Stated differently, modern good governance is to put people in the center of power, through civic awareness. And community organizing is the surest way to reverse a top-down governance style and to create an activator government based on true representation.

In true political representation, people have to voluntarily choose to be represented. They do so by organizing themselves and asserting grassroots-based influence on decisions that affect them. Information and ideas originate from the ordinary people and have an upward trajectory. You just can't get ideas imposed on people. People must feel the ownership of the process. At the risk of repetition, let me reiterate this point: Beware of imported politics in which the citizens are just the platform-fillers; that didn't work in the past and won't in the future.

Your role in community organizing is, henceforth, to be a catalyst who can midwife the realization of a community-driven power politics. I proved this point first hand. I taught the concept of community development and organizing for change for a couple of years and learned that a sense of power and belonging is created when communities respect each other and come together for a common cause. A class of 60 students was able to engage in a deeper way and to build an intellectual blood that separates them from others.

Now, five years after I took a break from teaching, I reached out to some of the class members, and each person I talked to was still connected to others. In a similar manner, grassroots democracy and community bonding can be taught to larger communities who would then come together to promote the common aim of all. Imagine a city that has this kind of bonding, connected not by the tribe but by intellectual blood.

Organizing your community takes effort, time, and a dedicated focus. It requires tailored plans and goals to shoot for, for a certain period of time. Your ability to organize your base is a vital step in your success, no matter your goals. You can't avoid this step and want to be successful in the people business. In fact, your future in politics depends on your ability to relate with others and mobilize your network toward specific objectives and goals. But the fundamental first step here is that there has to be a direction you'd like your efforts to take.

Keys to Communities of Practice

A government built by the few for the interest of the few, and led by the connected few, will always lack the legitimacy needed for a functioning democracy. If you're interested in participatory democracy in which the ordinary citizen can have the ability to co-design the form of government, you must invest in creating communities of practice and civil society machines. Indeed, the ultimate aim community organizing is to build communities of practice. That is the quickest route to civic involvement and politics that thrives on collective bargaining and ownership of the system by all. Communities of practice could be a lifetime goldmine.

Communities of practice take many forms and shapes. Some are nonprofits, some a hybrid of both. Whoever starts or finances them or their organizational structure, communities of practice are owned by the very community that would benefit from the organization's objectives.

Communities of practice are organized entities working to advance policies that have some relevance for the society they serve. Fundamentally, they're policy-driven and structured by by-laws and a common mission. And because of their connection with your target community, they're stakeholder organizations and well-informed about impending policies that are going to affect in their corner of the world.

Sometimes you've to create your own communities of practice. It's like if there's no ladder to the sky, build one. If you've to start your own communities of practice, be strategic and make sure that your communities of practice strive to have the capacity to organize people and ideas toward common goals.

The cornerstone of communities of practice is accountability. Successful communities of practice are owned by the people they serve, and are answerable to the very public that created them.

Even though public service is most associated with serving and representing people in government, professionals behind communities of practice are public servants, too. And they've to meet the same ethics, accountability, and integrity required of those in public offices.

Whether or not your community of practice or organization is funded by a particular group, you're in business to promote the interest of the public. Being accountable for whatever happens, whether everybody takes part in the initiative or not is the beginning of good governance and respect for the rule of law. Develop transparency and accountability systems will be inevitable, for the sake of a trust among indigenous communities of practice.

Communities of practice bridge the gap between what's and what should be. They do so by retailing in vision for the benefit of your communities and function as brokers of hope. They come in closing the gap between people of diverse needs by engaging in mediation and amalgamation. Needlessly, much of the efforts that fuel community organizing is based on bargaining in public and in private places.

Communities of practice help people to advance their interests and to make their cases at the table, individually and collectively. They create a place for others to assert influence on the decision-making process. Put differently, you and communities of practice are just facilitators of hope with no guarantee that you'll succeed in your endeavors.

Building communities of practice will require tremendous patience and passion for the trade. Practitioners may have to sustain long hours of work, standing on their feet for support. They visit people's homes and public gathering and talk with people who have every right to disbelieve them and their ideas. Moreover, it involves a back-and-forth movement where taking two steps forward and take another step backward is common. I believe that that comes with the territory and is a test for those who put themselves up for service.

There is strength in numbers, but organizing those numbers is one the great challenges.

Building a successful community of practice takes enormous resources, like time, energy, manpower, and the goodwill of everyone in the

community. That's why it's not a one-man business; it's a collective endeavor.
Doing the actual business of community organizing is an art similar to political organizing. You'll still need to mobilize, advocate for, promote, and sustain a large number of grassroots movements required for successful policy-oriented campaigns. John Mather wrote that the ideal community organizing lies in the power of the number of people mobilized, despite the challenges. According to Mather, "there is strength in numbers, but organizing those numbers is one the great challenges." This is when the act of building many communities of practice could make the difference.

Community organizing demands change agents with social and technical skills. In addition to the social skills required of politicians, change agents in community organizing are mini-psychologists who make sense of people's fears and hopes. They get to know people and acknowledge their concerns, dreams, and ambitions.

Principally, community organizing thrives on the idea of people taking ownership of the platform. People might not know the folks behind the platform, but they buy the idea of a common vision cast in a distant future. Agents are only facilitators; people are the drivers of the movement. Paul Wellstone stated that "successful organizing is based on the recognition that people get organized because they, too, have a vision."

Your role in organizing your constituency is, therefore, to create a platform where all can come together and discuss what matters to them. That means opening doors to everyone willing to participate in your community of practice and organization. Whether they agree or disagree with you isn't the issue here. The real issue is that people come together and talk, and talk endlessly without being judged or expected to leave their positions or viewpoints. If you're more open and receptive, people may lend you their hearts and trust. They'll give you the permission to lead.

Successful organizing is based on the recognition that people get organized because they, too, have a vision.

Once you create that inclusive platform, people will start coming in numbers. Two people, and then five people, and then ten people will come together. What had seemed impossible for an individual would now become possible.

But for this process of community organizing to work, a mandatory step is to create laws and defend those laws. Laws regarding liberty and people's desire to free expression and association should be created and upheld. Open democracy, the ability to express ideas publicly or privately and the freedom of assembly, sustain the lifeblood of all public discourses. And they're needed in communities of practice. That way people's desire to perfect their governance system is always upheld. Henry Louis Mencken, an essayist and a cultural critic, synthesized this point well when he wrote the following. "Democracy is the theory that the common people know what they want and deserve to get it good and hard."

> Democracy is the theory that the common people know what they want and **deserve** to get it good and hard.

In short, community organizing is the ultimate form of retail politics conducted in the most humane way. There's no place for egotistical politics in community organizing. It's a two-way street where open communication and face-to-face discussions are engaged.

A voluntary spirit to self-determination and co-shared density to face common challenges are important for the realization of a mature democracy. Actually, in democratic politics where people have the foremost voice in governance, a sympathetic listening to people's issues and concern is proactively sought out. Ideally, until people are able to form groups and hold conferences and meetings to attend their own issues, good governance is in jeopardy, democracy assassinated, and civic education buried.

But for such a process to materialize, community organizing must be based on higher ethical standards. As a catalyst, you should be totally honest with yourself, hold yourself to the highest standard, and people will give you the same in return. When things start to go south, only brutal honesty is a lifesaver.

As a rule, therefore, you're always better off with the naked truth than a tainted politics.

Colin Powell, a U.S. General and a former U.S. Secretary of State, put this concept brilliantly. "Honest, brutal self-examination is especially difficult, but even more vital after a mess, a screw-up, or a failing performance." Only when you're honest with yourself, can you be honest with others, including your stakeholders. As a rule, therefore, you're always better off with the naked truth than a tainted politics.

That's why community organizing is founded on a real truth, created within people and communities, not a rented truth. The real truth is one that's culturally and religiously appropriate and can't be distorted. It's attack-proof. Winston Churchill who was said to have maintained that kind of marry-the-truth attitude was quoted as saying: "The truth is incontrovertible. Malice may attack, ignorance may deride it, but in the end, there it is."

> **The truth is incontrovertible. Malice may attack, ignorance may deride it, but in the end, there it is.**

The real truth is commonly owned and invested in. You just can't sit in your office, shut the door, and dream of having truth slipping to you in the back door. Everyone matters in a country fragmented like Somalia. Indeed, my grandma in the jungle has a stake. You must be able to seek and bring her to the table. You're going to have to seek the most seemingly irrelevant stakeholder.

One unrivaled cousin of rented truth, and one you must pay a particular attention to, is deception. Deception happens when leaders are unhappy with a situation and resort to lies and misinformation because they lack integrity. Deception happens when a leader can't face the truth of his or her inability to see a better future for people but tries to maintain manufactured lies. Interestingly, deception and unethical behaviors are easy to spot in leaders who lack the self-confidence to represent themselves and their people.

Stay away from deception for it'll discredit your effort and lend an unquestionable power to those who oppose your ideas. You should never resort to unethical behaviors or thinking in this day and age when information is at the fingertip of anybody. Anybody can hop on the World Wide Web and find rich literature about anything.

Many people believe that politics is about hot deals of who gains the bigger pie, but that often involves a winner-takes-it-all approach. Zero-sum games don't work well in community-driven initiatives. Opt for a politics of shared consensus and avoid practices that lead to zero-sum games. Everyone in the community should be a winner, co-owning the governance system.

Give Power Back to People

Obviously, giving people the ownership of the entire community organizing initiative doesn't mean to create a bank of political positions for everyone, but the possibility of growth for all in the system. In order for you to change your community and face the challenges of your time, you must be willing to give power back to people, including those who disagree with you. You must never discriminate your opponents on the basis of their views, or suspicion of you.

Finally, the business of community organizing calls for agents who can get out of their comfort zones and are willing to show vulnerability. You're going to have to take risks and face uncertainty. That means putting yourself in the line of criticism and of appreciation.

The fact is, some people might not trust you, even though you're committed to their cause. Some won't even care about what you're claiming you care about. Worse, there's always going to be some people who will do everything to stop you or dismantle your mission and base. Some people will accuse of being a puppet, mad, and/or irrelevant.

Conspiracy theorists will follow you to your home and to your office exposing you to a higher level of vulnerability. Besides, there's always the danger of appearing foolish and rejected. That comes with the territory.

But the most astonishing part of this is that those who oppose your ideas and policies are those who need your community service the most. You must not lose focus. Remain confident in your people and avoid negative perceptions about your community, for that will hasten your downfall. You've to come across as a social change agent whose trustworthiness could be proven only by time.

If I were organizing in an orthodox Jewish community, I would not walk in there eating a ham sandwich.

You've to learn how to deal with both the layman, sophisticated people, as well as those who are in-between. Put differently, you must be a professional animal. Don't panic and don't lose your sanity. Even so, most people are gentle and understanding unless you cloud your reasoning and faith in them. Formulate your message as clearly as possible.

You must be patient and forgiving and be sensitive to people's cultures. Being sensitive to others means showing respect for their way of life, not upsetting people's orthodox views and ways of milking their cows. It means learning the ground rules, with regard to communities and groups. Saul Alinsky observed that every culture has some hardcore beliefs that are unshakable, that must be adjusted to. Saul wrote an intriguing statement. "If I were organizing in an orthodox Jewish community, I would not walk in there eating a ham sandwich unless I wanted to be rejected."

In your endeavors toward the realization of strong Somalia, challenges will become likelier than you're ready to believe. Don't give in to fear and uncertainty, lest you quit on your people and your nation.

Left Bank

Principle

4

Only measurable results keep ineffectiveness at a respectable distance.

"It takes an extraordinary intelligence to contemplate the obvious."

— Alfred North Whitehead, an English mathematician and philosopher

So, you're a leader, or at least you want to be one? I'm glad that you want to come forward and serve your country. But where are you going to go from there? Actually, a better question to ask is: How can I measure my leadership effectiveness? That's a great question, and every responsible leader should be asking him/herself.

For starters, leadership isn't about title, nor is it about the position you hold or would like to hold. Let's face it. Leadership is about what you do, and not the title you hold or intend to.

Effective leadership is not about making speeches or being liked; leadership is defined by results not attributes.

That's a practitioner definition of leadership. But when the word "effectiveness" is attached to leadership, the definition gets more complicated and harder to define. To make matters worse, most leadership experts observed that leadership is about influence over others and their actions, making the quantifiability of leadership even harder. Seriously, how could you measure your leadership influence and effectiveness? Because people follow your orders? Well, Adolf Hitler, the world's most ruthless dictator, had had a good followership and set the entire world in a different direction. People followed him not because they loved them but because they're so afraid to lose something that they enjoyed, whatever that might be.

Leadership is nothing but asserting influence on people and their actions. But what are the activities that lead to a successful influence and effective leadership? In the interest of precision, let's give two tentative definitions.

How many leaders have you reproduced?

John Maxwell, a leadership expert, defined leadership as nothing more but producing more people who could replace you when needed. Hence, Maxwell has a question for everyone who wants to claim the leadership title. He asks: "How many leaders have you reproduced?" In short, you ain't no leader if you're the only leader in the crowd. Your failure is certain if you're the kind of leader who believes that you're the only human cut to lead.

To Maxwell, leaders are in the business of duplicating themselves. Meaning, your primary task as a leader is to produce more leaders who could help you reach your potential and take over your job if needed.

Similarly, and with regard to effectiveness, Peter Drucker, a modern management guru, suggested that "effective leadership is not about making speeches or being liked; leadership is defined by results not attributes."

The principle in this chapter is, therefore, simple: your claim to effective leadership must be substantiated with measurable results. Whether they're working under a boss, or with a group, effective leaders are result-driven. They put their attention, and radar, on measurable results.

Leadership influence and effectiveness can be achieved through measurable performance. How can we measure our leadership performance? We do it by setting the right performance criteria in advance. Only measurable criteria can give us the results that we want, hence revealing our performance level, good or bad.

Criteria are nothing but benchmarks, telling us about our progress, or the results we want to produce so we know how effective, or ineffective, we're at the end of the journey. Practically speaking, here's a shot of how measuring the future performance of something works. We employ criteria when we inquire the year of the used car that we want to buy. We're using the mileage as a benchmark to predict if the car is reliable.

We all use numbers for a variety of reasons and situations. But critically, results are always preceded by highly defined criteria that can show whether we're producing the results we desired to achieve.

In a similar fashion, effective leadership is measured in terms of numbers, not how eloquent a leader is. That is, as Dr. Hermann Gottlieb once said, "numbers don't lie. Numbers are as close as we get to the handwriting of God." Hence, it's the measurability component of the equation that paves the way to understand if our claim adds up.

Numbers don't lie. Numbers are as close as we get to the handwriting of God.

We can't cut corners and bombard others with an empty talk and rented camera shots in the hope of disguising our ineffectiveness. Anyone can call the CNN International and ask one of the program anchors to put them on a live air. That's easy.

Unfortunately, as we head into the better part of the 21st century, you can't play with our perception and fool us. You're either producing results, or you're not. In short, only outstanding results can declare you an exceptional performer.

The sports legend, Michael Jordan, put how we could measure our performance in the most layman-like way. "If you don't back it up with performance and hardwork, talking doesn't mean a thing," Jordan wrote. In fact, the very reason that Jordan commands our attention, and respect, is that the man produces measurable results. His battings are just as measurable as our heights. Even if you don't follow his batting score in real-time, the number of scores under his belt isn't debatable.

If you don't back it up with performance and hardwork, talking doesn't mean a thing.

But it's not only Jordan's record that we can deduce some understanding of the science of effectiveness. Just as is true for individuals, the need to produce measurable results applies to groups, communities, and nations. Throughout history, the effectiveness of great leaders was measured by what they're appointed to achieve—results and nothing else. For example, the achievement of military generals was assessed and measured by how many decisive wars they had to win in order for them to be nominated into the effective leadership club. Presidents, prime ministers, and other public leaders were measured by how they grew their nations, not their bank accounts.

Similarly, the achievement record of educational leaders and teachers were measured against how many students they produced, who would then start meeting their individual and social challenges. A medical doctor's effectiveness was also evaluated based on the number of patients he/she had helped get back on their feet. In the same vein, business leaders were measured by quantifiable measures such as the profit they put into the pockets of their investors, the motivational level of their employees, and the products they bring to the market, among other things. What comes to your mind when you see Apple products? Steve Jobs. Why? I leave that to you.

The same performance measures apply to professionals in the public and social service sector. And as Mindy Grossman argued, "the proof is in the results, and the proof will be in the ongoing ability to execute." Meaning, effective leadership is in the proof, the measurability of our outcome. No one can dispute the outcome of 2+2. You can't expect 12, or 20.

The proof is in the results, and the proof will be in the ongoing ability to execute.

Sometimes the trouble lies in our activities to produce results. Unlike the era when leaders' actions were less public, how we set out to achieve effectiveness is as important as the results themselves. There's a public accountability measure that you need to meet. How you interact with your subordinates, the public at large, and the environment will also matter. Integrity is an all-time needed component of your strategy. Realistically, therefore, your actions and words must match before your effectiveness scorecard can be tabulated. This is so important because an unintended mistake can inadvertently stain your effectiveness record.

Fortunately, embracing result-oriented leadership is an art, and effectiveness can be achieved if the necessary work is chipped in. You can learn to lead by numbers, not by an empty talk, the province of the mediocre, the title-driven people who seek fancy dresses and extravagant events in order to look like a leader in the eyes of people.

On the one hand, those who fail to produce measurable results tend to look elsewhere to prove their worth. As a result, they buy the notion that a fancy dress-code might be a replacement for performance-based leadership.

On the other hand, effective leaders believe that effectiveness isn't an accident. To them, effectiveness is something that they control and decide to achieve. They set the effectiveness parameters for their workers and demand no mediocre achievements, and by the same token, set the bar for those who look onto them for help. Edmund Hillary observed: "people do not decide to become extraordinary. They decide to accomplish extraordinary things."

People do not decide to become extraordinary. They decide to accomplish extraordinary things.

Principally, when we begin to see the world from a quantifiable results perspective, we're well on our way to improving not only our chances to win but by the magnitude by which we're going to win. In the end, our attitude toward effectiveness starts to change, providing us with the confidence to lead scientifically. The idea is simple: In order to win, and win repeatedly, we must always be stretching, yearning for more, and then some more.

Above all, our tools must be sharpened at all times. We must constantly refine our thinking. Ultimately, the act of leadership effectiveness is to focus on the quantitative aspect of our claims.

Effective leaders aren't afraid of demanding others of acceptable results, and everyone around them is shooting for the moon. When you and your team are shooting for the moon, you've got a tractable system. If you could create that power, the power of casting your reality in front of people, you'll have an immeasurable edge and advantage that can put you ahead in the game of effective leadership.

On the flip side of the equation are the ineffective leadership and mediocre team players. Mediocre teams don't have enough picture of what they're expected of. They live on wishes and dreams. But result-oriented teams know the difference between wishing for something and walking down an uncertain path in order to maximize their chance of success. They can't sit behind closed fences and wish things were better. Doing so, they believe, is unethical. That's a right effectiveness concept, and Somalia must shoot for it in the years ahead.

Being ethical is about playing fair, thinking about welfare of others.

Effective leadership requires you to be truthfully ethical to yourself, to your people, and to the environment. Being truthful, honest, and squarely fine with results can be a good ethical practice. Katarina, Bogdan, and Metka asserted a thought that could capture this point better: "Being ethical is about playing fair, thinking about welfare of others and thinking about consequences of one's actions."

Research has proven time and again that we, humans, have the capacity to achieve effectiveness, but most people settle for a deadly comfort zone, writing off their chances of success. Without our noticing it, complacency sets in and becomes our silent enemy. As Jeremy Cutsche, a Canadian businessman, once said, "complacency will be the architecture of your downfall." This sure has been true of Somalia.

Complacency will be the architecture of your downfall.

Sometimes the results might not be realized quickly; it could be years before you see a light emerging. You may also face doubts and an ordeal process before you can see a glimpse of results beginning to add up on the horizon. In this case, patience is your personal assistance. Make no mistake, effective leaders are patient and mindful of the bigger picture. They know that the desired results may not come quickly. In fact, most worthwhile progress happens only gradually, and often when others start to lose faith in their leaders. If the prerequisite for effective leadership is measurable results, therefore, the prerequisite for measurable results is patience. Patience is a dealmaker, and those who are short of patience suck. No civilization or democracy can fix time and patience problems.

Leadership is crucial and vital in providing direction.

The hard truth is that nation-building processes take time and a tremendous amount of energy. Even so, there's no any guarantee that we'll end up producing the results we set out to produce. Effective leaders aren't afraid of losing. And when they fail, they fail effectively, because they are ready to learn from their failures.

Effective leaders are serious and frank about themselves and set ambitious goals for themselves and their nation. I don't believe that there's any drastic difference between setting SMART (specific, measurable, attainable, realistic and timely) goals for an individual, programs, or for a nation; setting SMART goals requires short- and long-range thinking and dedicated direction. According to Katarina, Bogdan, and Metka, there's nothing called effectiveness until goals and overall directions are set. They argued that "leadership is crucial and vital in providing direction that enables the organization to fulfil its mission and vision and achieve declared goals."

The more specific and measurable your goal, the more quickly you will be able to identify, locate, create, and implement the use of the necessary resources for its achievement.

Setting long-range goals are necessary, and as a leader, you're expected to set ambitious goals with deadlines, a timeline showing when and how you're going to achieve them. SMART goals specify the rules and provide a benchmark and a standard by which people will measure your success or failure. A measurable goal is one that's quantifiable. Let me throw an example. Suppose I say the following. "I'm going to produce 100 leaders by December 31, 2025." Now I've something specific that others can measure quite easily. I've, ab initio, the criteria against which my performance will be measured. By December 31, 2025, I either will have produced 100 leaders or I won't. Period.

Charles Givens, the bestselling author of Wealth Without Risk, gave an excellent advice regarding measurable goals. "The more specific and measurable your goal, the more quickly you will be able to identify, locate, create, and implement the use of the necessary resources for its achievement," Givens wrote in Wealth Without Risk.

Say, for the sake of argument, I actually trained and produced 80 leaders who can competently replace me at any time. Measurably speaking, 80 out of 100 isn't a bad deal. That's extraordinary as long as I intentionally wanted to achieve. With that, I'm keeping ineffectiveness at a respectable distance.

The good thing about setting SMART goals is that you put people in waiting. People, including outside your circle, will start counting the days to prove you wrong, perhaps. They start to patiently ponder how and by when you're going to achieve your SMART goals.

Some argue that it's challenging to measure good governance. There's some truth to that argument because setting measuring criteria and measuring the outcome may prove a bit harder. Unlike the SMART goal setting criteria—that have numbers attached to them—, building people's hopes and setting the standards higher for them isn't measurable either, as far as numbers are concerned.

We live in an era in which accountability and performance-based effectiveness are the driving criteria for good governance and civic democracy. Insisting on doing the right thing can put you on the fast track of a results-oriented world. In fact, if you've to take any message from this book, it's this: Only excellent performance can declare you an effective leader. And only measurable results

can keep ineffectiveness at a respectable
distance.

Principle

5

Three golden rules for Somalia's foreign diplomacy success.

"Success in foreign policy, as in carpentry, requires the right tools for the job."

— Richard Haass, president of the Council on Foreign Relations

President Mohamed Siad Barre's military administration did a lot of good things for this country, even though some doubted his diplomatic craft. In truth, though, President Barre did succeed in building a superior image tinted with power, influence, and respect, at least by measurable standards.

Somalia's reputation in the world reached a noble status during Barre's reign. But the issue that those who dispute this fact bank on is Barre's windy foreign policy. And I agree with them to some extent.

In an attempt to look different, President Barre projected an image of unpredictability and, as a result, attracted a huge misunderstanding among key global players of his time. Upset and, possibly, irritated, he started wearing many hats and jumped from one coalition to another. That's how this country got into the Arab League. Indeed, if President Barre made any foreign policy blunder, it's the act of making Somalia a member of the Arab League.

Somalia isn't an Arab state and can do better without the backup of egotistical Arab states.

Somalia shouldn't be a member of this dysfunctional entity for a number of reasons. For starters, Somalia isn't an Arab state and can do better without the backup of egotistical Arab states. Their ancient-smelling governance style isn't suitable for Somali.

Secondly, Somalia is an African nation. The only thing Somalia shares with the Arabs is Islam. I'm happy with that.

Somalia is an African nation.

History tells us that President Barre didn't believe in the Arabs and their friendship. Nor did he even have any confidence in how far Somalia could go with the help of the Arab League. Yet, he went ahead with the idea of making Somalia a poor member of that league. Other than that, President Barre did an excellent job. No doubt, the invention of the unwavering nationalism and civic education of the 1980s are a great example.

However, that status had been downgraded by our selfish desire to fight; the chase to grab for each other's throat led to an unprecedented disrespect for law and order. We tore the country apart, doing the most conceivable wrongs in the process.

The national hope for development and sustainable growth has been replaced by violence based on the desire of a few warlords whose aim in politics never went beyond bread. Thanks to the Islamic Courts Union (ICU) of 2006, the warlords were driven out of their strongholds. But sadly, a mediocre race for power is still active. We should collectively take responsibility for that.

The ensuing anarchy groomed a whole young generation unable to distinguish a commendable foreign policy from the poverty-oriented culture, the culture of dependence on aid. The nation's entire civilization dwindled, sliding the country back into the pre-Independence Era where poverty and tribalism were the main political socialization. Let me explain.

Since Barre's departure, Somalia has been engaging the world with a Somalia-needs-your-help mentality. In retrospect, those who came to power after Barre catered nothing but to their selfish interests. They pursued every conference in which the word "donation" popped up and made aimless trips to courting the big-pocketed, from east to the west. They couldn't even understand that the world is still separated by ideological lines. What happens when you court China, the U.S., and Iran all at the same time? You'll probably end up looking foolish, if you're lucky, let alone getting donations.

Because our leaders lost confidence in the ability of their nation, they approached the business of foreign relations with an inferior attitude—in part because poverty was ingrained in our minds. Their engagement with the world became assistance-oriented, the tendency to value aid assistance over long-term investments

Sadly, only those who were able to help the Villa to beg more were allowed to lead the nation's foreign service.

$160 Billion

That's why, since 1992, Somalia's entire GDP has been based on foreign assistance, which according to the World Bank totaled over 160 billion dollars by 2014. By now, you may be asking: Where did the money go? I've no idea!

The problem with Somalia foreign policy is that self-determination and national independence have been replaced by dependence on foreign help. The picture we tend to send to the outer world is one of entitlement. That Somalia can't exist without the continuous assistance of the west, and that we're entitled to that help. Ask any ambassador what he or she'd like to do, and you'll be showered with excuses of how Somalia would be better with huge sums of aid.

What our leaders don't understand is that foreign assistance doesn't lead to prosperity. It leads to the contrary, in fact. Foreign assistance makes people to become dependent on others not only for food but for thinking as well. When a nation begs, it inadvertently sells its intellectual heritage and becomes dependent on whomever donates the daily bread. Its citizens migrate to other advanced countries. Isn't that what we're witnessing today?

The principle here's that a responsible government doesn't beg other nations. Instead, a responsible nation sets policies that can attract investments and creates a win-win deal for potential investors. A responsible nation uses available technological tools and techniques to generate the most benefit and opportunity for its people and partners.

Competent nations operate from "our-interests-first" mentality. A good example is President Donald Trump's nationalist, "America first" slogan. Americans may disagree with Trump's tactics but not with the promise. Putting America's interests first isn't debatable across political aisles. What is debatable, however, is who can achieve that aim without making enemies, or having American soldiers in a foreign country.

The world of diplomacy has changed, but the tools of the trade haven't. The same old rules still apply, despite the technological advances. Nations always sought their interests aggressively, and there's always one way to subdue a nation, and whenever a nation seems defiant: diplomatic escalations and a possible war. No hearts to be broken. That's how the game of foreign relations has been, and will be, played. The old tricks, such as misinformation and propaganda intended to twist and manipulate the perspective of the world's exponentially increasing population, still apply.

Foreign policy is effectively the assertion of many individual countries intersecting on the global marketplace.

The sole business of any government is, therefore, to further the ideals of the country, without favor or affection. If the chief business of a nation's foreign service mission is to promote the values of that nation, diplomacy is the weaker nation's approach to seek cooperation from other nations.

Global-minded foreign policy initiatives anticipate other nations' interests and try to find a way to accommodate those interests. John Kerry, the 68th U.S. Secretary of State stated that "foreign policy is effectively the assertion of many individual countries intersecting on the global marketplace."

But the primary task of diplomats, and the overall foreign service of any nation, is to win the hearts of the citizens of the country they're assigned to. Because they're expected to communicate with diverse people, taking advantage of every opportunity and venue, diplomats are expected to be highly skilled.

If Somalia must get the attention of the world, hard choices are going to have to be made.

They're master negotiators who can communicate with a variety of people with different tastes. They appear on major TVs and radios of the countries in which they're stationed. They write regular columns and opinion pages. I vividly remember, while lived in Kenya, the U.S. and British ambassadors appearing in the Daily Nation, one of the major newspapers in Kenya, two days in a row. Those opinion pieces weren't mouthpieces. Every single word that the diplomats ushered was politically weighed to suit the current political issues and stances in the region. They were developed with great care, lest not to spark diplomatic panic in the hosting nation or a partner country. Most interestingly, both diplomats tried hard to convince the Kenyan people and the leaders about the positions of the U.S. and Brain in different ways.

The foreign policy of any nation represents the symbol of self-determination and national focus. Let's face it. Nations operate from the standpoint of leverage and comparative advantage. They focus on creating an arc of economic fronts, so they can negotiate from a position of strength and monopoly. What leverage does Somalia have? Zero! Most politicians are promoting the idea of shared security—that the world needs the cooperation of Somalia because of the religio-political conflicts in the Horn. That's a pedestrian thinking. Who cares if your home is burning?

Three Golden Rules

If Somalia must get the attention of the world, hard choices are going to have to be made. Somalia must define, and redefine, its foreign policy and an area of advantage on which the world is willing to partner with Somalia. The world must know Somalia's stance on virtually any issue, with clear goals and defined objectives. With that end in mind, I propose three golden rules that might lead to a successful foreign policy.

Rule # 1: Emphasize Investments

The first rule is simple: Emphasize long-term investments and not aid. Aid assistance is designed to work as a temporary relief, not as a substitute for long-term developments. Whether in the form of food, shelter or cash, training, or capacity building, the idea behind foreign assistance is to help the people in need to transition from poverty to recovery to development. That's why the longest aid program is set to run for five years or shorter. The USAID Administrator, Mark Green, wrote in the organization's premier news report: "The purpose of foreign aid is to end the need for its existence."

> **The purpose of foreign aid is to end the need for its existence.**

Somalia can approach the business of foreign policy differently right from the get-go. It can do so by tackling its security challenges and by removing obstacles impeding foreign investments and long-term economic plans. Instead of operating from a need perspective,

Somalia can take important strides designed to attract investors who can put the needed resources into the country's infrastructure for a decent return.

Those who have the money and the technology could be given the incentive to invest in the country. Think about the asset investments Saudi Arabia has in the U.S., the foremost developed nation in terms of economy and democracy, for instance. On its May 17, 2016 edition, USA Today ran a special report of the Saudi Arabian stake in the U.S. economy. According to the report, the U.S. Treasury disclosed that "the oil-rich nation was holding $116.8 billion" in U.S. economy.

Because of the oil in its region, Saudi Arabia has resources that most other nations need. That is why the U.S. is dependent on the Middle East oil, especially the reserves in Saudi Arabia. This is because investments are better than begging.

Now with that huge stake, no U.S. policy can intercede Saudi Arabia's deteriorating human rights record. Albeit the 9/11 Commission Report incriminated Saudi Arabia, both Bush and Obama administrations objected to any military action against Saudi Arabia. And Trump administration is unlikely to pursue a hostile policy against Saudi Arabia. Why?

Because the U.S. is dependent on Saudi Arabia. Indeed, the U.S. keeps its military base in Saudi Arabia just to protect its oil interests in the region. Saudi Arabia has something to capitalize on that the U.S. needs so badly. That's a perfect example of comparative advantage.

Somalia could replicate the same principles. Instead of buying cheap philosophies from the neighboring Muslim countries which couldn't help themselves, Somalia could have stood on its own feet and demand a fair chance of success through the pursuit of long-term investments. It could write new rules not only for itself but for others. That's possible.

Political motivations and incentives can be designed. No country ever neglected its foreign policy business and succeeded. Your leaders are fooling you if they're telling you otherwise. The chances are that they've been bribed to hide the facts and lie to you, all the while catering to the interests of others. The world can help Somalia on its own terms.

But real economic indicators must be developed. A skill-based economy should be the focus of any long-term strategic plan. What's more, for a real economic development to happen, people of working age must become self-reliance, depending on their rightfully earned paychecks. Lifetime skillsets are, for instance, some ways to reboot fully reliable income streams and dependable jobs and employment.

Rule # 2: Send Best Minds to Represent Somalia

Nations use their manpower and money wisely to manage the business of their foreign service. They send the best minds, men and women with special talents and passion for the job, to fool other nations. After all, the sole objective of a foreign service mission is to distract other nations from seeing the reality.

The goal is to blind them, so they don't see the opportunities in a common day. That's why Sir Henry Wotton, an English diplomat and a politician between 1614 and 1625, wrote: "An ambassador is an honest man sent abroad to lie and intrigue for the benefit of his country."

> **An ambassador is an honest man sent abroad to lie and intrigue for the benefit of his country.**

Beyond skills and the tools of the trade, these men and women are equipped with their nation's mission in the world. That's why, in its most basic form, foreign service involves selling the country's best image to other nations in the hope of attracting investors. A competent nation sends a consistent message to potential investors, although the goals and the overall direction that a nation is headed may change.

For the most part, self-determined nations have a way to secure their interests ahead of others'. That's to be expected in a world with scarce resources and greedy leaders.

Diplomats don't live on the premise of making money or getting pleasure for themselves, or for their bosses. Instead, these all-time busy servants burn their wheels by working on tight timeframes to serve their nation and serve it with an exception. They seek every opportunity to put the interests of their country ahead of everyone else's.

They don't engage in blah-blah in order to keep the leaders of their host nation happy. Instead, they manufacture and invent perspectives that help shape their part of the world, contributing to the national interests of their nation. They constantly shape the social discourse of their host nation. They're in constant communication with their bosses and with other colleagues in other countries. They're on the move, taking briefs from a variety of people, including their assistants.

A case in point is the U.S. foreign service mission. As of May 2013, there were 307 U.S. diplomatic missions (embassies, consulates, etc.) around the globe. That wider mission covers the entire 190 countries in the world. Of course, that excludes ten countries, such as Grenada and Iran, which the U.S. didn't have diplomatic presence or relations. Knowing the importance of foreign service business, the U.S. government maintains unofficial relations with these ten countries, normally through other embassies in friendly countries.

Somalia deserves a better place in the world.

That is why, the U.S. government kept its diplomatic relations with Somalia throughout the civil war and ran the operation from proxy states (e.g., Kenya). What does the U.S. want out of Somalia? you may ask. Friendship? Helping Somalia in the war against terror? B.S. As is evident in the preceding quote, Henry Wotton told the world four hundred years ago that the number one mission of every diplomat is to generate benefits for his or her country. Nothing else dominates the thinking of the most outstanding diplomats than how to get most out of the world.

Somalia deserves a better place in this interest-driven world. And that place must be built through diplomatic partnerships with friendly nations that can lend a helping hand to rebuild the nation. By a helping hand, I mean allies and friends who can invest in Somalia.

Rule# 3: Centralize Foreign Policy Operations
If Somalia can't afford a wider net of diplomatic presence, centralization of operations is an attractive option. With the right technology and technical know-how, Somalia can streamline its foreign operations under one roof, a single hub that filters everything that comes in and out of several nations.

Quiet diplomacy is far more effective than public posturing.

I believe that's what Atal Bihari Vajpayee, a former Indian prime minister, meant when he said that "quiet diplomacy is far more effective than public posturing."

In fact, nations with the most means do use that tactic for a variety of reasons, and Somalia can do the same to its advantage. There's no need to stretch your budgetary ability just to look big. What is the point of showing off when you're spoon-fed by other nations?

If Somalia is to be respected in the global community again, it must rethink and re-examine its national and regional goals. It must decide its national interests and prioritize those interests accordingly, so it doesn't need to chase every political friendship and alliance.

Instead of sending sloppy men and women who lack the necessary diplomatic vigor, Somalia should look for to attract and recruit the best servants, train them in relevant skills, and send them to foreign stations. The bottomline is that these servants must be capable to actively play on a competitive global stage. Their goal should be clear: Somalia's first, partner nations' second.

That doesn't necessarily mean that Somalia resorts to negative attitudes, or that it looks at the world with an angry eye. But whatever the route to diplomacy, Somalia must avoid traveling the beggar's road. Doing so will lead your nation to a hell of constant poverty, incompetence, and mediocrity. In the end, you produce a state suffering from diplomatic constipation.

Understand: When you send a diplomat, who thinks that his or her mission is to beg for the boss, the entire nation is marginalized. That's true when you send a diplomat who believes that powerful nations write plans for the powerless.

Diplomatic constipation happens when a state sends a diplomatic representation to another nation and asks the hosting nation to pay the bills of its diplomatic service. That hosting nation maybe probably eager to take care of your bills, but you must realize that you've become part of their plans. That nation will own you for life because it's feeding your diplomats; your representation becomes a token used against your nation.

Conversely, when a nation embraces the road of self-determination and independence, that nation automatically looks like a partner in the eyes of other nations. Do the opposite, and you'll automatically join the club of inferiors and beggars.

Principle

6

Tribalism divides our hearts, nationalism unites our morals.

"I think, tribalism is a mental prison…and pride of identity coupled with arrogance is one of the leading factors that limit one's ability to abandon it."

— Duop Chak Wuol, Editor-in-Chief of the South Sudan News Agency

Whether social, political, or economic, there're always roadblocks that stand between a nation and its dreams. Some nations face security challenges; some are seriously struggling with financial setbacks. And yet others are confronted with perennial issues that are transferred to and inherited by subsequent generations. However, the degree of self-determination a nation asserts in dealing with its contemporary challenges can make a decisive difference.

Somalia has been held back by one stinky plague that impeded progress since its founding. That's tribalism, the mother of all ills. You think about of security, economic, social, and political challenges and you simply are taken back to that stinky leveler. It eats not only the nation's social capital but also divides our hearts. In many ways, tribalism is the primary enemy of Somalia. And it'll continue to face it until appropriate policies to dealing with tribalism are put in place.

Tribalism corrupts our morals and creates disrespect for the rule of law.

The Dark Sides of Tribalism

Think of tribalism as the number one enemy that stands in your way, and that you're going to have to fight it on your way to effective leadership and self-determined Somalia. Actually, tribalism is the ugliest roadblock for young politicians. They must confront it or risk social stagnation and probable failure.

Tribalism corrupts our morals, creates disrespect for the rule of law, and destroys the human capital, the hard currency of any nation. It keeps many talented people below the poverty line. Have you ever seen young men and women with advanced degrees who are unemployed, or underemployed, because of their tribe? They couldn't make it to the interview stage because no one could do the secret handshake or the backdoor deal for them. That's just a tragedy as terrible as hell. Abshir Nuur Faarax (Bacadle), whom admire so much for eloquent poetry, was right when he said, "wax qabiil kadaran jahannabaan qiray aqoontayda."

Wax qabiil kadaran jahannabaan qiray aqoontayda.

Tribalism spells a disastrous plague when educated men and women remain unemployed because the guy in power is from another tribe. Our hearts are broken and divided forever when someone has to be burned to death for loving someone. That's a culture that needs to be abolished.

Tribalism is an agent of chaos, my friends. Period! It destroys the goodwill of the entire nation of Somalia. It destroys the hope and faith that people might have in each other and in those who govern them.

In a cycle as old as tribalism, ignorance of the other engenders fear; fear engenders hatred; hatred engenders violence; violence engenders further violence.

Those of us who came of age during the 1990s know the cost of tribalism: lack of opportunity and destruction of moral judgment. Somalis went to war with each other in the 1990s, and thousands of young men were recruited into armed groups and lost in the process. Those who survived are still struggling with remnants of the tribalism, not to mention the lack of access to good education and economic opportunities.

Whether you want to admit it or not, tribalism still keeps the nation apart. Dark stairs of tribalism are stacked on the horizon for many inspiring individuals. David Mitchell described the result of unrestrained tribalism. He wrote: "in a cycle as old as tribalism, ignorance of the other engenders fear; fear engenders hatred; hatred engenders violence; violence engenders further violence until the only 'rights,' the only law, are whatever is willed by the most powerful."

For many, tribalism has been, and still is, an ego-booster. Deep down, people who use tribalism want to express their loyalty to something that can't satisfy the greater good. They use it to satisfy their inner insecurity and moral deficiencies. Marty Rubin confirmed this tendency in the Boiled Frog Syndrome. According to Rubin, "tribalism is really a form of egoism. It's all about my people, my religion, me, me, me." Now, Somalis across the board seem to be dancing "me, me, me."

Tribalism is really a form of egoism. It's all about my people, my religion, me, me, me.

When a man loses his morality and resorts to tribalism, the result is corruption, twisted moral judgments, and ultimately social death.

Absurdly, tribalism went deeper into our head until we justify it in the Quran.

Tribalism is a destructive concept imported from the Arabian Peninsula and put, like a sausage, in the fundamental history of Islam. Prophet Mohammed, all blessings be upon him, took advantage of the social fabric and tribal affiliations of the early 7th century Arabs. The modern teachings of Islam with regard to nationhood were rooted in the strategies Prophet Mohammed employed to spearhead his campaigns to ground Islam in the Arabian Peninsula. That's how tribalism was *sausaged* into Islam. I don't want to go into details about the pros and cons of the 7th-century tribalism. But suffice it to say that non-Arabs, including myself, confuse Islamic history with the Islam itself.

Absurdly, tribalism went deeper into our head until we justify it in the Quran, perhaps, the wrong way. People who are committed to tribalism use the following Quranic verse, usually interpreted the wrong way. "O, you men! Surely We have created you of a male and a female and made you tribes and families that you may know each other" (49:13). To many people, people were created of tribes in order for them to know each other and to distribute resources accordingly. I'm not qualified to discuss this topic, but suspect that this is the most pedestrian thinking you'll encounter in the social realm across the nation. God never created people to commit human rights crimes against other people.

I'm not suggesting that there's an issue with this verse, or that it should be tweaked to suit our meaning or desires on earth, or just by virtue of hating tribalism. I'm merely referring to the idea of people deepening tribalism in the Quran itself. I'm only bringing your attention to the fact that your number one enemy has the backup of your own faith. That's just my thinking. (I ask God for forgiveness whenever I'm wrong.)

The idea behind the principle in this chapter is that we should understand tribalism and its cancerous impact on the socioeconomic nerve of the entire nation. We must treat it as we'd treat a person with a quickly spreading cancer. When a person contracts a brain cancer, there's only one logical method that medical doctors throughout the world advice: the removal of the dead tissue. Tribalism is a dead tissue, and we must isolate it by cutting its roots, for there's nothing we gain by entertaining tribalism.

Let me be clear. There's nothing that I hate more than tribalism and those who promote or defend it. Right or wrong, that's who I am. I'm prepared to take a firm stand whenever someone slips tribalism into the normal conversation. I follow my instincts and can sense tribalism from a distance. And you can do the same if you want to quarantine the virus.

How to Eradicate Tribalism

If you want to eradicate tribalism, you must be unshakable. You must immunize yourself. I believe Margaret Thatcher, one of the most powerful stateswoman the world ever saw, communicated this point well. "Don't follow the crowd, let the crowd follow you," she advised. Instead of letting virus-carriers into your life, you're better off eradicating the roots of the virus by getting tribalists out of your life.

Tribalism never prospers.

Let's be frank with ourselves. What good does tribalism have for us? Zero! As the British-Czech Ernest Gellner wrote, "tribalism never prospers." No matter how you look at it, the present tribal system in Somalia has no value proposition for the people and the country. You're terribly mistaken if you believe otherwise.

Tribalism is a serious and complicated disease, and its eradication is going to require painful preparations. More so if you're striving for a more ethically realistic social system. And if you're honest about growing people, people must feel the ROI in their lives and constituencies.

And you're unlikely to think far ahead into your strategic outplay of nation-building if you've an enemy sitting at your door. You're better off dealing with it quickly and decisively. Cut off its roots once and for all. The following three tips are helpful to deal with it effectively.

Tip # 1

The best advice I've for you is this: Never associate with virus-carriers. Simply eliminate from your circle those who willfully insist on participating in tribalism, or even propagating it directly or indirectly.

You must understand people's motives; be a mini psychologist. Why are your friends hanging out with you? Because they feel that you belong to their special tribal web? Are they meeting you over coffee or lunch because they want to deepen their tribe-based relationship with you? Tribal affiliations kill human talent and eat away people's intellectual worth and creativity. You must develop the feeling to sense it from a distance.

A Meeting with a Virus-Carrier

Not long ago, I found myself in a situation where I had to deal with a virus-carrier, a person who passed my initial screening as a hardheaded professional. One evening, I stepped into a restaurant in Minneapolis, Minnesota, USA, for dinner only to find two men, a friend whom I'd not seen for a while and another man. After a few jokes, my friend suggested that I should connect with his friend. We agreed, set an appointment, and departed.

Can I ask you a question?

Then came the date of our meeting, and we finally met. "Can I ask you a question?" he said right off the bat.

I gave him my complete attention, in order to make sure I wouldn't miss the point of this serious-looking guy. But to my dismay, what he asked put me off. "What is your tribe?" he threw up!

I decided to leave quickly because I wasn't willing to waste my precious time entertaining a tribalist in the heart of the Midwest America. I excused myself, headed toward the bathroom, and took the backdoor exit, never to meet him again. In retrospect, I'm so glad that he started off with that question, for that question told a lot about him.

> **I'm for truth, no matter who tells it.**
> **I'm for justice, no matter who it is for**
> **or against.**

That's me for you. My official tribe is truth vested in professionalism, justice, and equality before the law. That means a lot more to me than tribalism does. Malcolm X was reported to have said: "I'm for truth, no matter who tells it. I'm for justice, no matter who it is for or against. I'm a human being, first and foremost, and as such I'm for whoever and whatever benefits humanity as a whole."

That must be your criteria toward good ethical standards. You don't need to succumb to tribalism and pedestrian thinking by allowing virus-carriers into your life. Stand clear and think on your feet. And the whole world will respond to that positive vibration that you're sending. Put differently, it's better to be known for a nerd than for a tribalist.

It won't take long for people to realize your free spirit and relate to you accordingly. In fact, it's much easier for people to relate to you, once they understand your philosophies and uncompromising ethical judgments.

But before you reach that status, be prepared for ridicule and teasing. Those who benefit from tribalism will work harder, so you can come to their level and commit to their causes. Whatever the situation, never compromise your values and philosophies but remain steadfast, instead. And like Thomas Jefferson, the 3rd U.S. President, once said, "in matters of principle, stand like a rock; in matters of taste, swim with the current."

In matters of principle, stand like a rock; in matters of taste, swim with the current.

The point is, you must develop a thick skin as you confront tribalism. Keep your composure and be polite at all times.

Tip # 2

Avoid any tribal gratitude that might drag you into difficult terrains but remain neutral in your interaction with people. People will remind you of some gratitude that they bestowed upon you, or your great-grandfather, sometime in the past. The idea is to get inside your skin and make you emotional, so you can lose your consciousness and judgment. When you lose your conscious judgment and become irrational, you become a victim of tribalism.

Being conscious and awake can help you in understanding and filtering who's on your team. If you're not extra alert, a stubborn fellow can easily distort your consciousness. Play the big picture principle and never let virus-carriers to compromise your moral health.

Tip # 3

Have a system, a protocol, that can help you get a healthy crowd for your mission. More so, building a nation requires building a new kingdom of friends and compatible environment based on worldviews and like-mindedness, and not tribal affiliations. Those new-found friends will concur with you and help you in creating the kind of democracy that you envision for your nation. Those same friends will widen your network connecting

you to their networks, and network of
networks.

Leave high school and stop majoring in the minors.

This system, if you work it right, will be the
immune system that might protect you from
contracting the virus of tribalism. You want to
know whom you can depend on from who can
dismantle your vision. Because the stakes are
high, you can't let the virus to dismantle your
system.

For Somalia to make a measurable progress
toward a democratic society where
relationships are based on mutual trust and
respect, we all have to leave high school and
stop majoring in the minors. With the finest
team and a plan to work with, you can create a
tribal-free form of governance that works for
all, many, many years to come.

At this point, you might ask: How can I know
virus-carriers from others? Honestly, tribalism
is like a dead body; it stinks, and you can
smell it from a relatively respectable distance
if you pay a careful attention. Yet, the most
straightforward way of detecting tribalism is
to sit back and observe, always scanning your
environment. Tribalism has symptoms. Read

its symptoms so you can keep the virus at bay before it spreads in your system. This tactic can be of an enormous help to you as you build your network.

But for this technique to work, you must know how to control your emotions at will. You'll be lured to participate in people's dirty fight and arguments. Never throw yourself into conversations that groups are having among themselves. Never let yourself be dragged into a fight of not your choosing. People will reveal to you who they really are. Never intervene in others' affairs; wait for them until they reveal themselves.

A leader without moral principles is like a ship floating in an unstable wave.

Finally, you might be tempted to swim with the current social status quo. At all cost, stay true to your cause, use your moral compass to guide your decisions, and cultivate good moral principles for a leader without moral principles is like a ship floating in an unstable wave. You'll be beaten before you produce the results you're after if people question your moral character. You're better to be known for an anti-tribalism nerd than be known for a wishy-washy fellow who swims in the tides of clanism as a pendulum.

When you refuse to follow the mediocre, you're refusing to let the bad ideas that kept Somalia in the dark alley of chaos and disorder to impact you. You're creating the politics of possibility for the first time. Otto von Bismarck, a German statesman between 1860 and 1890, said that "politics is the art of the possible, the attainable—the art of the next best." You're shooting for the stars.

Principle

7

Ethical leadership isn't a choice, it's the right thing to do.

"Trust is the essence of Leadership."

— Colin Powell, former United States National Security Advisor and Secretary of State

The hallmark of competent leaders is ethics. In fact, if there's anything that separates good leaders from bad ones, it's this: Good leaders exemplify excellent ethical leadership throughout their careers. They understand that a higher ethical standard isn't a situational undertaking. Or something that they can drop and pick up at will.

Contemporary ethics can be defined as doing the right thing, thinking the right stuff, behaving right, and acting constantly in a matter that does no harm to all living beings, even when circumstances are against us, or no one is watching. Ethical leaders believe in integrity, that their actions and words match in an integral way. It's been said that "integrity is doing the right thing, even if nobody is watching."

> **Integrity is doing the right thing, even if nobody is watching.**

Because they're biased toward higher ethical standards, ethical leaders choose to functionalize the part of the brain that scans out the bad thinking. In his book, Meeting the Ethical Challenges of Leadership: Casting Light or Shadow, Craig Johnson, an emeritus professor of leadership studies at George Fox University, Newberg, Oregon, wrote, "ethical thinking activates both cognitive and emotional areas of the brain." Ethical leaders control not only their situations but how things could be interpreted. Everything they do, don't do, comes out of a choice.

The practice of ethical leadership is a two-part process involving personal moral behavior and moral influence.

Leaders aim for higher moral grounds in all their undertakings, in order to achieve ethical results. Simply put, ethical leaders believe that appropriate behaviors can set the tone for the right leadership. And they want to exemplify it for their followers. Johnson observed: "the practice of ethical leadership is a two-part process involving personal moral behavior and moral influence." Meaning, and as the Swedish proverb goes, "in calm water every ship has a good captain." Ethical leaders are good captains of a responsible ship. It's been said that people follow leaders not because they have to but because they need to.

The other side of the coin of ethical leadership lies unethical leadership. Unethical leadership is deemed to be the act of outright selfishness. All selfish people inhabit in the I-don't-care-about-others region. They've no faith in people and have less regard for people's welfare.

According to Gordon Graham, the author of Eight Theories of Ethics, "selfish people in this sense are people who (for instance) always try to get the best seat, or the finest steak." As a result, unethical leaders always work from the premise of deceit and manipulation.

Selfish people in this sense are people who always try to get the best seat, or the finest steak.

Dishonest and manipulative behaviors are the hallmarks of unethical leaders. They've a grandiose sense of egoism and selfish motives that cloud their ability to make sound decisions. They overlook the fact that leadership is a human transaction between different stakeholders whereby all—leaders, followers, and variety of others—are mobilized to achieve a common goal.

The reason that ethics is so important in leadership is that leadership is about influence, and influencing people in the wrong way is highly costly. How those in leadership positions behave or think is going to have an enormous impact and influence on the outcome of the entire process, including how subordinates behave.

That's why good leaders choose an excellent ethical standard in the first place. They know that people rely on them for everything, including moral support. For them, behaving ethically isn't an accident; it's a choice. All ethical leaders throughout history made the decision to be ethical. In his book, Leadership Theory and Practice, Peter Northouse observed: "the choices that leaders make and how they respond to in a given circumstance are informed and directed by their ethics."

> **The choices that leaders make and how they respond to in a given circumstance are informed and directed by their ethics.**

While what constitutes moral decision-making can be hard to pinpoint across cultures, ethical leadership can be easy to identify from unethical ones. Similarly, despite right and wrong might be debatable across cultures, wrong and harmful behaviors are easy to spot. This is in part because the common denominator of all unethical behaviors is harm.

Unethical leaders have an odor that can be felt from a distance. Their thinking is ego-propelled, and behaviors deceit-charged. If you glance at the history of the most recent global economic crisis, especially the last one in 2008, you'll realize that it all started with the executive leaders' chronic sense of egoism, the primary threat to making sound, ethical choices.

What often corrupts the mind of most promising leaders is their desire for fame. Fame alone can act as an intrinsic motivator to achieve unethical ends through whatever means. Ethical leaders, in contrast, put their personal desires aside and work from the idea of inclusivity and accountable teamwork.

Ethical principles require that leaders to put their egos aside and to lead from their heart because leaders' characters and hedonistic tendencies can cloud leader's moral judgment, if used improperly, or left unchecked. When leaders lie, and leaders steal from the public, communities suffer, and the nation starts to lag behind its promises.

The key challenge today is how to meet the last two—trust and ethics.

In its most fundamental form, therefore, leadership is a process wherein leaders learn the skills of making ethical and moral choices and face the challenges, both classical and contemporary.

In leadership, there's no finish line but successive steps to climb, requiring adjustments to make, and it's during climbing these steps that leaders are tested. Fred Hilmer, an Australian academic and former president and vice-chancellor of the University of New South Wales, presented the key must-haves in exemplary leadership. He wrote that "leadership requires five ingredients—brains, energy, determination, trust, and ethics. The key challenge today is how to meet the last two—trust and ethics."

In Somalia, leaders lie just about everything, and as a result, trust is an issue. In the past, they lied about the international aid intended for the needy, and the military assistance they had received from foreign nations. They faked stories and invented red-herrings for those who bribed them.

They justified their immoral behaviors and misplaced their responsibility in order to avoid blame; and they misinterpreted the current realities the nation faced, in order to look good. All these issues contributed to the deficit of truth and quality leadership. The result? A complete failure of moral imagination and disengagement. A political greed crept up onto the public psyche and caused moral chaos across the board.

When the public thinks that political deceptions and looting of national resources are the normal state of affairs, shifting the social narrative isn't easy, but it's doable. And ethical leadership can be a crucial determinant of success. Hopefully, in Somalia where, moral disengagement, blatant lies, and deception are the order of the day, ethical leadership can make a difference.

The good news is that the current unpromising status quo can be turned around. We can build a new leadership formula based on respect for all and propensity toward catering to the common good. We can, once and for all, replace Somalia's current tribal-based leadership credo with principled ones—humility, optimism, courage, justice, and compassion. These character-based qualities represent the credo of all responsible leaders.

Leadership consists not in degrees of technique but in traits of character.

Lewis Lapham, writer and editor of the American monthly Harper's Magazine, declared: "Leadership consists not in degrees of technique but in traits of character; it requires moral rather than athletic or intellectual effort, and it imposes on both leader and follower alike the burdens of self-restraint." It's apparent that ethical leaders develop the discipline to control themselves.

Ethical leaders don't shy away from seeking the truth. They seek reality and the grounding truth no matter who has it. They attract followers who help them in producing the truth they need. They're always asking: Who's likely to disagree with us? And in this question, they're not seeking naysayers but challengers who can poke holes in their thinking.

> **Leadership is the art of giving people a platform for spreading ideas that work.**

They're in search of good ideas and innovative ways to better the lives of those whom they lead. And in so doing, they extend their scope by reaching out to others, both friends and foes. According to Seth Godin, an American author, "leadership is the art of giving people a platform for spreading ideas that work."

Ethical leaders put their people first. Putting people first is a noble character that all ethical leaders must possess. In fact, people don't care about your title that much; they want to be cared for. President Theodore Roosevelt was quoted to have said, "people don't care how much you know until they know how much you care."

People don't care how much you know until they know how much you care.

Ethical leaders don't just look at things and make up their mind. They consult with their followers and weigh all the options before taking action. They rally their followers around the shared choice of action. That creates a power of leadership mix where both leaders and followers sustain the momentum for the benefit of all. Warren Bennis said, "followers who tell the truth, and leaders who listen to it, are an unbeatable combination."

Ethical leaders understand that they'll be deemed unethical in the long-run if they choose to entertain bogus thinking. That's why, in the back of an ethical leader's mind, is the question: Is this going to hurt anyone? Best of all, they're inclined to take an alternative route whenever they're unsure about the answer to that question.

Ethical leaders have a system built over the course of their working lifetime that filters out immoral thinking, and subsequent actions. This systematic approach to decision making

                    Abdiqani Farah

helps them in identifying unethical elements in any decision, big or small.

Habits of Ethical Decision Making

Years of research has identified six habits that lead to clever, ethical decision making. These habits are (1) leading with the end in mind, (2) doing things in the right order, (3) seeing the big picture principle and thinking of win-win, (4) seeking to understand the situation fully by inviting all involved to reflect on the problem at hand, (5) creating a collaborative and synergetic environment, (6) and sharpening "the saw." These habits can put leaders onto the fast track of becoming excellent in their fields.

> **Followers who tell the truth, and leaders who listen to it, are an unbeatable combination.**

Ethical leadership requires that we approach every decision systematically. The idea is that we can't implement ideas that comes to our mind without the employment of proper techniques and filtering lens that can help us in spotting the ethical issues involved. Johnson presented some powerful techniques, checkpoints with regard to decision making: (a) recognition of problems, (b) determining the actors of these problems, (c) gathering all facts before decisions, (d) testing right against wrong, (e) testing all values, (f) employing ethical standards, (g) seeking the third option, and (h) making the final decision. He concluded that ethical leaders are systematic and "take a systematic approach to moral reasoning."

In short, the moral reasoning of ethical leadership is based on humility, justice, and compassion, which helps other traits of good leadership come into play. Overtly ethical leaders have courage, temperament, seeking wisdom, optimism, integrity, reverence, among other things, ingrained in their subconscious mind.

Indeed, moral reasoning and ethical decision-making can be learned and mastered through practice and imitation, and ethical leaders are proactive in their choice to be ethical. They're continually crafting extraordinary leadership characteristics and building their morality around their molding personality, so they emerge as morally competent individuals who consciously seek and adopt good moral reasoning.

In sum, ethical leaders are flexible and willing to take a step back and self-examine themselves, lest their egos stand in the way of ethical decision making. After all, with every moral decision made, leaders are sharpening their ethical skills by learning from their mistakes.

Ethical leaders are prepared for life's hardships and aren't terrified by mistakes and failures, personal and professional setbacks, and other traumatic in life. Actually, ethical leaders are responsible enough for themselves, just as they're for the world around them, and they discipline themselves to welcome hardships and suffering. With every challenge thrown in their way, ethical leaders are willing to work on their mistakes and to perfect their moral standing. In Failing Forward, John C. Maxwell made an important assertion. "If a weakness is a matter of character, it needs much attention. Focus on it until you shore it up," he wrote. For an ethical leader, a mistake is a chance for character building.

Ethical leaders have their integral characters in writing, and they're willing to communicate their message in a variety of ways. One way to communicate their message is through a goal-focused mission statement which tells their followers, and the rest of the world, who they're. That is, the mission and the complete focus of ethical leaders' orbit are built around stories, well-told stories that are reflective of experiences shared by all including subordinates.

What matters is grounding stories that bind together their mission and their people's expectations; however, the absence of resonating stories can lead to premature decision making. Johnson argued that ethical leaders "impart values and encourage self-discipline, caring, and other virtues through the telling of narratives or stories."

Technically, ethical leadership emphasizes putting a moral hat on from day one; doing so to take the first step toward effective thinking and leadership. "Effective leadership is putting first things first," according to Stephen Covey. And for Somalia, putting in place a leadership that believes in ethical and higher moral judgment is a principle worth pursuing.

Effective leadership is putting first things first.

Thank you for reading this book.

This book is dedicated to all who care about Somalia. If you liked it, please recommend a friend.

Abdiqani Farah

abdiqanieau@gmail.com

Thank you, again.